INSPIRATIONAL CHRISTIAN STORIES FOR 8 YEAR OLD BOYS

FAITH-FILLED TALES OF COURAGE, HONESTY, AND KINDNESS

Published by
GRAPEVINE BOOKS

www.grapevinebooks.com
email: contact@grapevinebooks.com

Ordering Information:
Quantity sales: Special discounts are available on quantity purchases by corporations, associations, and others. For details, reach out to the publisher.

First published by Grapevine Books 2026

A LETTER, JUST FOR YOU!

Hello, adventurer!

You are growing, learning, and figuring out who you are every single day. Sometimes that feels exciting. Sometimes it feels like too much. You might face moments where you wonder if you are brave enough, strong enough, or good enough.

You are. And these stories are here to remind you of that.

Inside these pages, you will meet boys who mess up, get back up, say the hard thing, do the right thing when nobody is watching, and learn to trust God even when life gets complicated. None of them are perfect. But every single one of them discovers that God shows up anyway. You will find Bible verses, prayers, and challenges to carry the message into your actual life, not just leave it on the page.

You were made on purpose, for a purpose. Every step you take toward courage, honesty, and kindness is a step toward becoming exactly who God had in mind when He made you. That boy? He's worth knowing.

Let's go!

TABLE OF CONTENTS

SHOW UP ANYWAY

Theo had a system for visiting Papa Joe.

Step one: grab the good markers, not the dried-out ones that looked full but were basically lying to your face.

Step two: pack three chocolate chip granola bars. One for Papa Joe, one for himself, and one emergency backup in case the first two disappeared mysteriously, which they always did.

Step three: do not, under any circumstances, forget the drawing pad.

The drawing pad was important. Papa Joe had always loved Theo's drawings. Even back when Theo drew horses that looked like potatoes with legs, Papa Joe had studied each one like it belonged in a museum and said, "*Now THAT is a horse, Theodore. That horse has character.*"

Nobody else called him Theodore. Just Papa Joe.

That was before.

"Ready?" Mom called from the bottom of the stairs.

Theo sat on the edge of his bed and stared at his drawing pad. It was the thick one ninety-six pages, slightly dented on the corner from the time he'd dropped it on the dog. Bruno *still* looked mildly offended about that.

"In a minute," he called back.

He wasn't ready. He hadn't been ready in about six weeks, which was roughly how long ago Papa Joe had looked at him and said, with total cheerfulness: "Hello there, young man! Are you Margaret's boy?"

Margaret was not Theo's mom. Margaret was apparently someone from Papa Joe's childhood who had once won a pie-eating contest and never let anyone forget it.

Theo was not Margaret's boy.

He was *Papa Joe*'s boy. Everybody knew that. Papa Joe had taught him to fish, to whistle through two fingers, and to always check under the car before backing out because "that's where the cats sleep, Theodore, and cats have opinions." They'd watched old Westerns together every Saturday for as long as Theo could remember, sharing a bowl of popcorn and arguing about which cowboy was the best one.

(Papa Joe said Clint Eastwood. Theo said the cowboy from the cereal box. Papa Joe said that wasn't a real cowboy. Theo said the cereal was very good so it counted.)

And now Papa Joe didn't know his name.

> **Psst. Before we go any further...**
>
> Has anyone you love ever changed in a way you didn't expect? Maybe they got sick, or moved away, or just... became different somehow. Here's a challenge: think of one thing you still have with that person, one thing that hasn't changed.

The Sunridge Memory Care Facility smelled like floor cleaner and, faintly, like cinnamon rolls, which Theo had decided was either the best or worst combination in the world, depending on the day.

Mom signed them in at the front desk. Theo carried the drawing pad under his arm and tried not to make eye contact with Mrs. Patterson in Room 4, who always wanted to show him photos of her seventeen grandchildren and he could never remember which one was Gerald.

Papa Joe's room was at the end of the hall. Room 11. There was a small corkboard on the door where the staff pinned things like a photo of Papa Joe from years ago, a handwritten card, and a printed piece of paper that said

"Joe loves: John Wayne movies, lemon drops, and his family."

Theo had written that. Back in September, when everything was different.

He stared at it for a second. Then Mom knocked and opened the door.

Papa Joe was sitting in his armchair by the window, looking out at the parking lot with the focused expression of a man watching something extremely important. He was wearing his red flannel shirt, the one with the slightly-too-short sleeves that made him look like he'd borrowed it from someone, and he had a half-eaten lemon drop on the table beside him.

"Joe," Mom said warmly. "Look who came to visit."

Papa Joe turned. His face lit up: that big, rumpled smile that Theo had known his whole life, the one that made his whole face crinkle like paper.

"Well!" Papa Joe said. "Company! Sit down, sit down. Don't just stand there like a lamp."

Theo sat.

There was a pause.

Papa Joe looked at him pleasantly. "You know," he said, "you remind me of my grandson."

Something in Theo's chest did a slow, terrible drop. Like an elevator with a broken cable.

"Yeah?" Theo managed.

"Theo." Papa Joe nodded seriously. "Good boy. Strong drawer. Made me a horse once. Best horse I ever saw." He picked up his lemon drop, considered it, put it back. "You look just like him, you know."

Mom made a small sound. Theo didn't look at her.

You look just like him.

He was him. He was sitting right there, in the same jeans, with the same drawing pad, three granola bars in his backpack and his whole heart sitting on the floor of Room 11.

This was a mistake. He doesn't know you. Coming here doesn't do anything.

He wanted to go home. The Worry-Engine (that's what Theo called the thing in his chest that started clanking and hissing when things went wrong, like an old boiler about to blow) was running at full speed.

THE BRAVE CHOICE:

Theo is about to make a decision. Before you read on, here's yours: write down (or just think about) one person in your life who might need you to show up even when it's hard. You don't have to do anything yet. Just name them.

Theo opened his drawing pad.

He wasn't sure why. His hands just did it while his brain was still arguing with his chest.

He picked up a blue marker and started drawing a horse. Not a good horse. A very bad horse, on purpose, with four wobbly legs, a head shaped like a sock, a tail that looked more like a question mark.

Papa Joe leaned forward.

"Hm," he said.

Theo kept drawing. He gave the horse a cowboy hat. Then a tiny lemon drop, because why not.

Papa Joe made a sound that was not quite a laugh but was cousin to one. "That horse," he said slowly, "has *character*."

Theo's marker stopped moving.

Those exact words. The same words. Like something that lived so deep in Papa Joe it couldn't be forgotten, not by whatever was happening in his brain, not by any of it.

"You think so?" Theo said. His voice came out a little croaky, like a frog who'd been sitting in a cold pond too long.

"Absolutely." Papa Joe was nodding. "That horse is *somebody*."

Theo drew another horse. Then a cowboy. Then a horse AND a cowboy. Papa Joe watched every single stroke with the same expression he'd always had – interested, pleased, like he was being let in on something good.

For forty minutes, they sat together. Papa Joe didn't say his name again. He called him "son" twice, which wasn't right but wasn't wrong either. Once he asked Theo if he liked lemon drops and Theo said yes and Papa Joe gave him the last one from the dish and said, "Good man."

Theo ate it. It tasted like lemons and something he couldn't name.

> Love that doesn't ask to be remembered is still love. It might even be the biggest kind.

On the way home, Mom was quiet for a while. Then she said, "You okay?"

Theo thought about it. The Worry-Engine had slowed down. Not off, but quieter.

"He said the horse had character," Theo said.

Mom glanced over. "I know."

"He always said that."

"I know."

Theo looked out the window at the trees going past. November trees, bare and a little dramatic, like they were posing for a sad painting. He thought about Papa Joe in his flannel shirt, leaning forward in his armchair, watching a wobbly crayon horse like it was the most important thing in the room.

He didn't know my name. But he knew I was somebody worth talking to.

Maybe that was something.

His Sunday school teacher Mr. Addo had read them something once. Theo had been half-listening because Marcus had been making increasingly ambitious paper cranes in the back row, but one line had stuck like a burr to a sock:

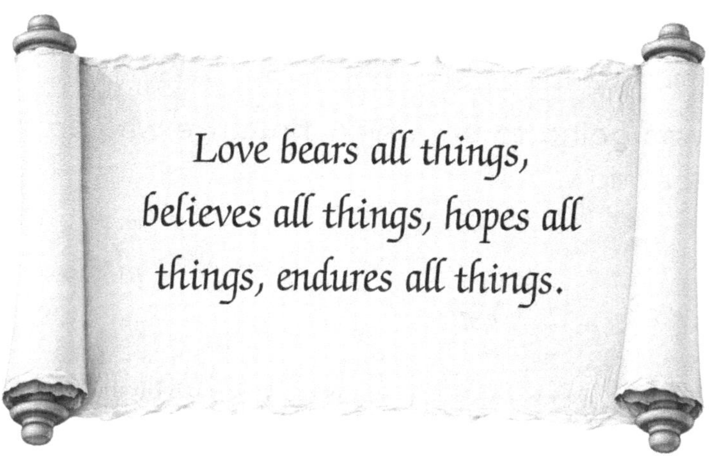

That night, Theo drew one more horse. This one was better. Not potato-legged, not sock-headed. Proper legs, proper mane, a good strong nose. He gave it a cowboy hat and a lemon drop. Then, at the bottom of the page, in his best handwriting, he wrote:

For Papa Joe. From his grandson Theodore.

THE DRAWING DARE:

Theo showed love without words, using just a marker and a drawing pad. Your challenge: this week, do one thing for someone that has nothing to do with words. Draw something, make something, fix something, leave something. No explanation needed. Just do it and see what happens.

He left it on his desk. He wasn't sure what he'd do with it yet. Maybe bring it next time.

There was going to be a next time. He was pretty sure about that now.

Theo didn't get his name said. He didn't get recognized. He didn't get a hug with the right name attached to it. And he still came back. That's not a small thing. That might actually be one of the bravest things in this whole book.

A PRAYER FOR YOU

God, sometimes the hardest kind of missing is when the person is right in front of you. Thank You for the parts of people that don't disappear, like the way they laugh, the things they love, the look in their eyes when something makes them happy.

Help me keep showing up even when it's hard. Help me love without keeping score. Help me remember that You love me the same way: without conditions, without a list, without ever forgetting my name. Even on the days I forget Yours. Amen.

THE HARDEST PRAYER YOU'LL EVER SAY

Isaiah had a name for the feeling Tyler Pemberton gave him.

The Boiling Pot.

It started somewhere around his stomach, this slow, low heat that crept upward whenever Tyler was within twenty feet of him. By the time Tyler opened his mouth, the Boiling Pot was already at a full bubble, and Isaiah had to clench his jaw and remind himself that his dad had specifically said that knocking someone's lunch tray onto their own shoes was not a conflict resolution strategy.

Tyler Pemberton had hair that defied gravity in a way that seemed deeply unfair, and had been making Isaiah's third grade year the approximate equivalent of stepping on a Lego. Every single morning.

It started in September. Tyler had looked at Isaiah's sneakers on the first day of school, pointed, and laughed loudly enough that six other kids turned around.

They were perfectly good sneakers. They were just not the right brand, apparently, according to Tyler, who was eight years old and had somehow already developed opinions about footwear that belonged on a person three times his age.

Then came the lunch situation.

Isaiah's mom packed him the best lunches. Not fancy, just good. A sandwich, some chips, a fruit cup, and occasionally, if it was a great day, a pack of the little chocolate cookies with the cream in the middle. Tyler started sitting two seats down and making comments. Not loud enough for the teacher to hear. Just loud enough for Isaiah.

"Ooh, fruit cup. That's sad." “Did your mom pack that? Cute." "Nice sandwich. Very ... *kindergarten*."

Isaiah had a running mental list of Tyler's offenses, organized by category, which he felt said a lot about how much he could not stand Tyler Pemberton.

REAL TALK, BEFORE WE GO ON:

Everybody has a Tyler. Maybe yours isn't at school. Maybe it's on the bus, or at practice. You don't have to like them. But here's a question: do you know anything about why they are the way they are? Just something to think about. We'll come back to this.

The Wednesday it all boiled over started normally enough.

Isaiah was eating his lunch, working through his chips, when Tyler knocked Isaiah's fruit cup off the table. *Not* by accident. Tyler made a very specific movement with his elbow, made eye contact with Isaiah as he did it, and then looked away like nothing had happened.

The Boiling Pot hit maximum temperature.

Isaiah glared at him. Tyler looked back with the innocence of a cherub. Their lunch monitor Mrs. Gaines materialized between them with the speed of a woman who had done this before and was tired but professional about it.

Both boys ended up in the principal's office. Tyler claimed it was an accident. Isaiah said it wasn't. The principal sent them both back to class with a warning that used the word "behavior" four times in two sentences.

That evening, Isaiah sat down to dinner with the specific energy of a thundercloud that had been asked to please calm down and had strong opinions about that request.

His dad noticed immediately. Dad always noticed. He had what Isaiah privately called the *Dad Radar*, which could detect a bad day from forty feet and through walls.

"Okay, talk," said Dad, setting down his fork.

Isaiah talked. All of it. The sneakers, the lunch comments, the fruit cup, the principal's office. He talked for six straight minutes, which was a personal record, and by the end he was gesturing in a way that knocked his napkin off the table.

Dad listened to all of it without interrupting. Then he sat back, crossed his arms, and said something Isaiah had absolutely not anticipated.

"Pray for him."

Isaiah stared. "I'm sorry?"

"Tyler. Pray for him. Every night this week."

THE SEVEN-DAY DARE:

Isaiah's dad just gave him a challenge that sounds simple and is actually one of the hardest things in this book. Is there someone you'd secretly be okay with having a bad day? Try saying, out loud or in your head: "I hope they're okay today." Even if you don't mean it yet.

"Dad." Isaiah said it the way you say someone's name when they have suggested something that makes no scientific or logical sense. "*Dad*. He knocked over my fruit cup. On purpose. While looking at me. I want God to deal with him."

Dad's mouth twitched. Not a smile exactly. The thing before a smile. "What does 'deal with him' mean?"

"I don't know. Something unpleasant. Nothing serious. Just embarrassing."

"Isaiah."

"I said nothing serious!"

Dad picked his fork back up. Isaiah opened his mouth. Closed it. Looked at his green beans. He could feel his Dad, or rather, both of his fathers, judging him.

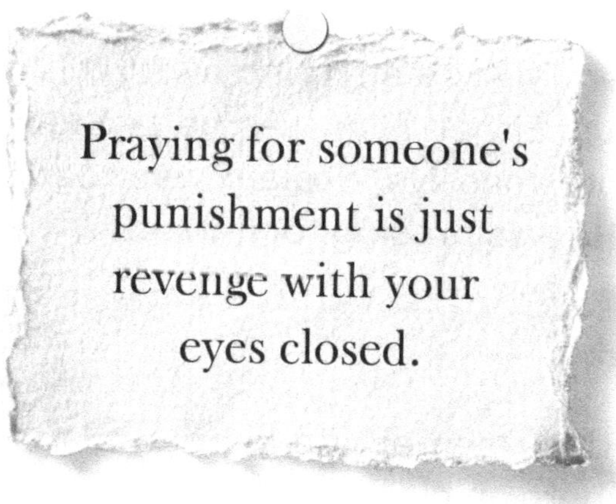

He groaned. "*Fiiine*. What should I do instead?"

"Pray for him to be okay," Dad said. "Not punished. Not embarrassed. Just okay. Can you try that? One week."

Thursday night, Isaiah prayed for Tyler. It went like this: "God, I am praying for Tyler Pemberton. Like Dad said. Amen."

He felt exactly *zero percent* better.

Friday night:

"God. Tyler Pemberton. Again. You're *welcome*. A-*men*."

Saturday night he accidentally fell asleep halfway through and dreamed Tyler knocked over a very large fruit cup in slow motion, which Isaiah felt was not his fault and probably didn't count against him.

Sunday, Monday, Tuesday. Each prayer slightly longer. Each one feeling slightly less like talking to a wall and slightly more like talking to someone who was actually listening, and possibly trying not to laugh at him.

He hadn't seen Tyler do anything awful this week, which was suspicious. Either Tyler was behaving or saving up for something massive. Isaiah was betting on the second one. He was bracing for impact.

It didn't come.

Instead, on Friday, something happened that Isaiah had not put anywhere on his list of possible outcomes.

He was walking back from the bathroom during free reading time, padding down the hallway in his regular sneakers, when he saw Tyler.

Tyler was sitting on the floor against the lockers, knees pulled up, face down. His shoulders were doing the thing shoulders do when someone is crying and trying extremely hard not to look like it.

Isaiah stopped.

He stood there for about twelve seconds.

This was not part of any plan. The Boiling Pot was very confused. It had been prepared for a fruit cup incident. It had not been prepared for this.

CHALLENGE: WHAT WOULD YOU DO?

Stop here for a second. Genuinely. If you walked past someone who had been making your life miserable and they were sitting on the floor looking like that, what would you do? Walk past? Stop? There's no wrong answer. (Or ... is there?)

Isaiah thought about walking past. He thought about it seriously, with genuine intent, for about four of those twelve seconds.

Then something his dad had said surfaced in his brain without permission. Not even from this week.

From a Sunday morning a while back, when Isaiah had been mostly paying attention during the sermon and his dad had leaned over and quietly said: "You know that part in Matthew where Jesus says to pray for people who make your life hard? He wasn't suggesting it."

Isaiah had said "okay Dad" and gone back to his bulletin.

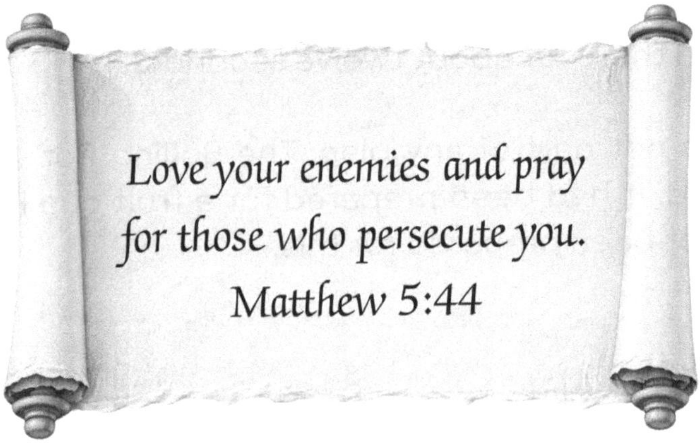

Now, standing in the hallway looking at Tyler Pemberton trying not to cry against a row of lockers, it landed differently.

He walked over. He sat down on the floor. Not right next to Tyler. A normal, non-weird amount of distance away.

Tyler looked up. His face did several things in quick succession: surprise, then embarrassment, then the automatic scowl that was apparently his face's default emergency setting.

"What do you want," Tyler said. Not really a question.

"Nothing," Isaiah said. "Just sitting here."

Tyler stared at him. "Why."

"Because the hallway floor is surprisingly comfortable."

It wasn't. It really wasn't. It was cold tile and Isaiah was *fairly* certain he was sitting on a dried piece of something that had once been a sticker.

This might be the worst idea I have ever had.

But he stayed.

Tyler looked away. After a minute his shoulders did the shaky thing again, and he said, very quietly, "My grandpa's in the hospital."

Isaiah didn't say anything for a second. *Oh*, said something inside him. Not the Boiling Pot. Something quieter.

"That's really bad," Isaiah said. Because it was. There wasn't a fancier version of that. Tyler didn't answer. But he didn't tell Isaiah to go away either.

They sat there together for three minutes, on the cold tile floor with the dried sticker and the faraway sound of someone's classroom doing multiplication tables, and then the bell rang and they both got up and went back to class without another word.

That night, his prayer was different.

"God, I hope Tyler's grandpa gets better. And I hope Tyler's okay. He's still annoying. But I hope he's okay." He paused. "Also... thank You for the cookies with the cream in the middle. They are genuinely excellent. Amen."

On Monday, Tyler sat one seat further down at lunch and didn't say a single word about the sandwich.

Praying for someone doesn't mean what they did was okay. Isaiah still had every right to be upset about the fruit cup. The sneaker thing was still rude. None of that disappeared. But somewhere between Monday night and Friday afternoon, Isaiah stopped carrying Tyler around like a heavy backpack full of bricks. That weight is exhausting. Putting it down doesn't mean the other person wins. It means you get your energy back.

A PRAYER FOR YOU

God, I'll be honest with You. This one's hard. There's someone who has made things really difficult for me, and my first instinct is not to pray for them. My first instinct is... not that. But I'm trying. So here it is: I hope they're okay. I hope whatever is going on inside them gets better. Help me carry less anger and more peace. And if You ever want to explain why loving enemies is supposed to be a thing we do, I'm listening. I trust You know what You're doing. Amen.

BRAVE ENOUGH FOR ONE MORE STEP?

Samuel had a very specific opinion about thunderstorms.

They were fine. Totally, absolutely *fine*, and anyone who said otherwise was being dramatic, and Samuel was not dramatic. The fact that he slept with a nightlight was entirely unrelated to storms and was simply a personal preference that he had held since he was four.

His little sister Abby, on the other hand, had no such composure.

Abby was five years old, roughly the size of a golden retriever, and operated at approximately the same emotional volume. When things were good, Abby was very good. When things were bad, Abby was a siren. An actual, human, non-stop siren with pigtails.

Tonight, things were bad.

It had started fine. Mom and Dad had driven to Nashville,

Nana Mae was in the guest room at the end of the hall, and Samuel was in his bed reading a comic book about a robot who fought volcanoes. A solid way to spend a Friday. Abby had conked out at eight o'clock.

Then the storm arrived.

Not politely. Not with a little patter of rain and a distant rumble. This storm showed up like it owned the place, slammed the door behind it, and immediately started making itself at home. Lightning split the sky in half. Thunder rolled in so low and heavy that Samuel felt it in his molars.

He sat up in bed. To nobody, he said, "That's fine."

Then the power went out.

> **QUICK QUESTION, FROM ME TO YOU:**
> Have you ever been scared of something but tried to act like you weren't? Maybe in the dark, maybe somewhere new, maybe in front of someone younger than you? That pretending you're fine thing, it's exhausting, right? Keep that in mind as you read.

The room went from dim to absolutely, completely, zero-percent-lit black. Samuel's nightlight, which ran on electricity and had never let him down before in his life, was gone. Just *gone*.

Samuel sat very still.

He was not scared. He was simply taking a moment to assess the situation in a calm and rational manner, like a person who was completely fine.

Then Abby screamed.

A full, committed, top-of-the-lungs, wake-the-neighbors-if-there-were-any-neighbors-within-half-a-mile scream. The farmhouse was surrounded by fields and the nearest neighbor was a cow named Gerald, but Gerald probably heard it too.

"SAMUELLLLL!"

Samuel was out of bed before he'd decided to be.

He grabbed the flashlight from his nightstand, the one his dad had put there specifically for power outages because his dad was the kind of person who planned for things, and clicked it on. A beam of yellow light cut across his bedroom floor. He stood in it for one second, two seconds, breathing.

She's calling your name. You have to go.

His feet disagreed. His feet had a different suggestion, which was to stay right here in the bedroom where the monster-to-Samuel ratio was currently a very comfortable zero-to-one.

Thunder hit again. The whole house shook. Something rattled in the kitchen.

"SAMUEL PLEASE."

He went.

THE BRAVE-O-METER

Bravery is not a zero or a one. It's not either "fearless hero" or "hiding under the covers." There's a whole middle section. Samuel's feet didn't want to move. He moved them anyway. Where are you on the Brave-O-Meter right now, or in life?

The hallway was dark in a way that hallways really commit to when the power goes out. Samuel swept the flashlight left and right like he'd seen people do in movies, which helped about fifteen percent. Every shadow looked like something that wasn't there. The storm was hammering the roof. The windows were bright white every few seconds with lightning. And Samuel was moving through all of it on two legs that were doing their absolute best.

Abby's door was already open. She was sitting up in her bed, both arms out, face soaked, making the sound of someone who had recently decided the world was ending and wanted everyone to be informed.

"I'm here," Samuel said. "I'm here, Abs." She latched onto him like a koala who had been told this was the last tree on earth.

Samuel sat on the edge of her bed and let her, even though her grip on his arm was genuinely impressive for someone her size.

"It's so loud," Abby sobbed. "Make it stop."

"I can't make it stop," Samuel said. "It's a storm. It has to stop on its own."

"TELL IT."

"I'm not going to tell the storm to stop."

"Why not."

"Because I'm eight, not a weatherman."

Abby thought about this for a moment. Then she buried her face back in his arm.

Another crack of thunder, longer this time, like it was rolling across the whole state of Tennessee just to make a point. Abby made a sound that Samuel felt in his own chest.

He looked around the room. The flashlight made a small warm circle in all the dark. Rain was hitting Abby's window so hard it sounded like gravel. The curtains were the ones with the little ducks on them, which looked significantly less cheerful in lightning flashes than they did in daylight.

Samuel did not know what to do. He was eight. He was not equipped for this. He was equipped for comic books and cereal decisions and occasionally feeding the chickens. He was not equipped for being the only person standing between his little sister and a Tennessee thunderstorm.

He wished Nana Mae would wake up. He thought about going to get her. He almost did.

And then, from somewhere in the part of his brain where Nana Mae's Sunday morning voice lived, a sentence arrived.

Nana Mae had a habit of saying things at breakfast that stuck to you whether you wanted them to or not. She said them the same way she passed the biscuits, casually, like it was nothing, and then they just sat there in your brain taking up space.

A few Sundays ago she had looked at Samuel over her orange juice and said, "Isaiah 41:10, baby. That's the one for when you're scared. Write it on your heart."

Samuel had not written it on his heart. He had eaten his biscuit and thought about the robot volcano comic.

But apparently it had gotten in there anyway.

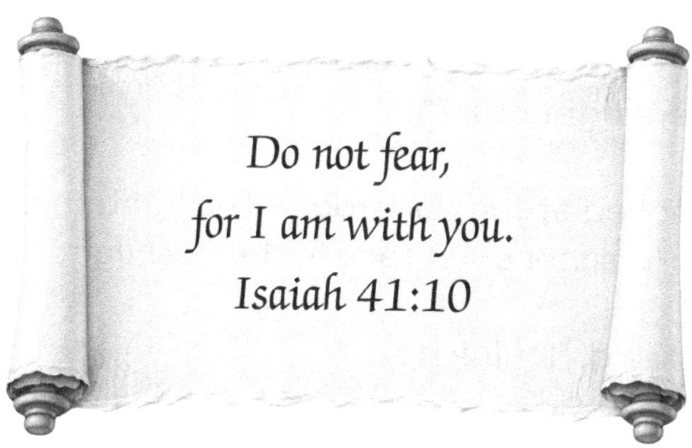

Something in his chest shifted. Not a big shift. Not a movie-moment shift. Just enough.

> **ARE YOU GONNA BE BETTER?**
>
> Can you memorize Isaiah 41:10 before you finish this chapter? Seriously. Read it three times right now. "Do not fear, for I am with you." Six words. See if it's still in your head by tomorrow morning.

"Abby," Samuel said. "I'm going to say something. You have to listen."

"I don't want to listen, I want the storm to stop."

"I know. Just listen anyway." Abby made a noise but she was listening. Samuel could tell because the koala grip loosened slightly. "Do not fear," he said, "for I am with you."

Abby sniffled. "Who said that?"

"God did. Nana Mae told me."

"Is God here right now?"

Samuel looked at the dark room. The lightning. The duck curtains. His sister's wet face in the flashlight beam.

"Yeah," he said. "I think He is."

Abby considered this with the seriousness of a five-year-old weighing important information. Then she said, "Say it again."

He said it again.

And *again.*

By the fourth time, her breathing had slowed. By the eighth, the storm had started to pull back, the thunder moving further away like something that had made its point and was satisfied.

They sat together until the rain became a murmur.

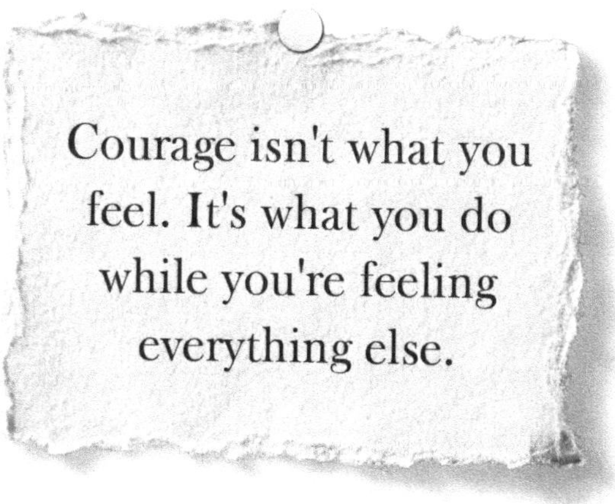

Nana Mae appeared in the doorway at six in the morning, hair in a braid, slippers on, holding two mugs of hot chocolate with the focused expression of a woman who already knew everything.

"Heard you two had a night," she said.

"We were fine," Samuel said.

Nana Mae looked at him over her mug. One eyebrow up.

"Mostly fine," he said.

She handed him a mug. Then she sat in the little chair by Abby's window and looked out at the washed-clean morning, the fields all glittery and the sky a pale washed-out pink. Abby was still asleep, burrowed under the covers like a small determined mole.

"Isaiah 41:10," Samuel said, after a while.

Nana Mae looked at him. "Yeah?"

"It works."

She smiled the kind of smile that takes up her whole face. "Told you to write it on your heart."

"I did," Samuel said. "*Eventually.*"

You're going to have your own dark hallway someday. Maybe you already have. Maybe it's not a storm, maybe it's something harder than a storm, something with no lightning and no thunder, just a quiet kind of scary that sits in your chest and doesn't make a sound. This is for that too. You don't have to feel brave. You just have to move your feet. God goes with the feet, not the feelings.

A PRAYER FOR YOU

God, I don't always feel brave. Honestly, sometimes I feel the opposite of brave, like a coward. So I'm asking You tonight: go ahead of me into the dark parts. Not just the power-outage kind of dark. The kind I carry around. Help me remember that You said "do not fear" like You meant it, because You did. Help me move my feet even when my chest is loud with scared. And if there's someone smaller than me who needs me to show up, help me show up. Amen.

BE THE ONE WHO SPEAKS UP

Marcus had a very simple rule about recess: Whatever happened on the playground, stayed on the playground.

This was not a rule his parents had taught him, or his teacher, or anyone in an official capacity. It was just something Marcus had figured out through careful observation and two years of elementary school experience. Recess was its own world. Different rules applied. You could fall off the monkey bars and get up and pretend it didn't happen and nobody said anything. You could lose spectacularly at four square and walk back to class like a champion. What happened at recess was between you, the blacktop, and God.

He had not, until today, considered that the *God* part was actually serious.

It started with Leo's yo-yo.

Leo had brought it in against the rules, which both of them knew, which was exactly the kind of thing Leo did, because Leo had what Marcus's dad called "selective rule awareness," meaning Leo was very aware of rules he liked and considerably less aware of rules that got in the way of a good time.

The yo-yo was electric blue with a yellow lightning bolt on the side and it lit up when it spun, which Marcus had to admit was genuinely cool. They'd spent most of recess taking turns with it on the covered walkway outside their classroom, which was also against the rules but was at least indoors, which felt slightly more responsible somehow.

"Watch this," Marcus said, winding it up.

"Don't throw it too hard," Leo said.

Well. Marcus threw it too hard.

The yo-yo launched off the end of the string at a speed that Marcus would later describe, in his head, as "scientifically unreasonable." It crossed the walkway in approximately *zero* seconds, hit the classroom window, bounced off the glass, and struck the corner of the fish tank sitting on the low shelf just inside the open classroom door.

There was a sound.

Not a crash exactly. More like a deep, ceramic groan, followed by a crack, followed by what Marcus could only describe as the fish tank making a decision.

The decision was: *leak*.

Not a trickle, either. A committed, enthusiastic pour of water that spread across the shelf and began its journey toward Mrs. Rivera's reading corner carpet with the confidence of something that had somewhere to be.

Comet, the class goldfish, circled once and looked confused. Which was fair.

HOLD ON A SECOND.

Before Marcus has to figure out what to do, you have to figure something out too. Imagine this: you just broke something by accident. Nobody saw it happen except your best friend, who is currently making a face that means please don't involve me. What do you do first?

Marcus and Leo stood in the doorway and stared at the spreading puddle.

"Okay," Leo said.

"Yeah," Marcus said.

"That's bad."

"Very bad."

"Maybe it'll stop."

It did not stop.

Comet was now swimming in about two inches of water and starting to look genuinely stressed, which Marcus felt was relatable.

"We should tell someone," Marcus said.

Leo turned to look at him with the expression of a person who has just been suggested something completely unreasonable. "*Or*," Leo said slowly, "we could go back to the playground. And when Mrs. Rivera comes in she finds it. And nobody knows."

Marcus looked at the puddle. The puddle looked back.

"What about Comet?"

Leo picked up the small plastic cup from Mrs. Rivera's pencil holder, dumped the pencils onto the desk without ceremony, scooped Comet out of the tank, and held the cup up. "Comet is fine."

Comet swam a small, indignant circle.

"We can't just leave," Marcus said.

"We absolutely can," Leo said. "Our feet work. The playground is right there."

And the thing was, standing there in the doorway with the water spreading and Leo holding a very unimpressed goldfish in a pencil cup, it did sound possible. Easy, even. Nobody had seen them. Mrs. Rivera was at lunch duty. The rest of the class wouldn't be back for four minutes.

Marcus's feet pointed themselves toward the playground almost automatically.

MARCUS'S BRAIN: A WEATHER REPORT

Currently experiencing: heavy pressure from one best friend, light drizzle of guilt, seventy percent chance of bad decision. Proceed with caution.

They made it back to the playground. They played on the swings for the remaining three minutes of recess and did not look at each other. Marcus pumped his legs and stared at the sky and felt something growing in his chest that he did not like.

It showed up whenever he did something he knew was wrong and tried to pretend he hadn't. It had appeared once when he'd blamed his sister for eating the last of the cereal when he'd done it himself. It had appeared the time he'd told his mom he'd brushed his teeth when he hadn't.

It always showed up. And it never left until he fixed it.

The bell rang.

Mrs. Rivera found the tank at the same moment the class filed back in. She saw the puddle, the cracked glass, the shelf dripping steadily onto her carpet...

Comet sitting in a pencil cup on the desk wearing an expression that can only be described as "done with today."

"Oh goodness," Mrs. Rivera said. She said it quietly, which was somehow worse than if she'd said it loudly. Then she turned to the class. "Does anyone know what happened?"

Twenty-two children looked at the tank. Then at each other. Then at their shoes.

Marcus looked at Leo. Leo looked at the ceiling. He had apparently found something very interesting up there.

Nobody knows, said one part of his brain. *You're fine. Stay quiet. This blows over by tomorrow.*

And then, without his full permission, his father's voice arrived. A quiet Tuesday-morning kind of voice, the way his dad talked when he was saying something that mattered but didn't want to make a big deal of it. Marcus had asked him once why he always told the truth even when it was inconvenient, and his dad had looked at him and said, simply:

> God sees either way.
> Might as well let
> Him see you doing
> the right thing.

Marcus had been seven when his dad said that. He was eight now.

Apparently one year was long enough for it to take root.

> **RIGHT HERE. THIS IS IT.**
>
> The moment Marcus decides is coming up. But before he does, here's your challenge: write down the name of one time you stayed quiet when you should have said something. You don't have to show it to anyone. This is just between you and the page. And maybe God.

Marcus raised his hand. "Mrs. Rivera," he said. "It was me. I was playing with Leo's yo-yo on the walkway and I threw it too hard and it hit the tank. Leo didn't do anything wrong. It was me."

The room went very still.

Twenty-two children stopped breathing at approximately the same time. Leo, who had been studying the ceiling, slowly looked down.

Mrs. Rivera looked at Marcus for a long moment. Her face was unreadable in the way that adult faces sometimes are right before they do something you don't expect.

Then she said, "Thank you, Marcus."

Marcus had been prepared for a lot of things. He had prepared for disappointed voice. He had prepared for a note home. He had prepared for a sad head shake and possibly a lecture that would last until Thursday. He had not prepared for two words delivered in a tone that sounded almost like she was grateful.

"Class," Mrs. Rivera said, turning around, "we're going to spend ten minutes helping clean this up before we start math. Marcus, you can help me move Comet to the big bowl in the supply closet."

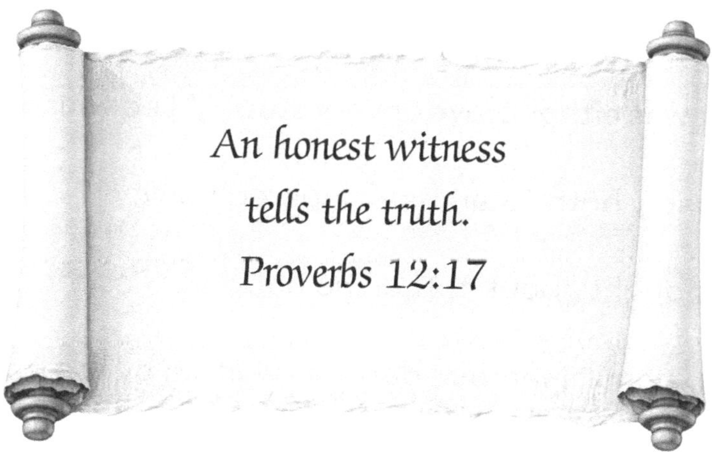

Marcus nodded. He picked up Comet's pencil cup. Comet looked up at him with the blank, round eyes of a fish that had been through something.

"You're okay," Marcus told him quietly. He was pretty sure he was talking to himself.

By the time the puddle was gone and Comet was circling his temporary home, the whole thing felt less like a disaster and more like something the class had solved together. And at his desk, Marcus noticed something.

The space in his chest where his guilt had been sitting felt lighter than it had in a long time, like a window had been opened in a stuffy room. He hadn't expected that.

> That peace in your chest after you do the right thing God saying: "well done!"

“That was either brave or very stupid," Leo whispered.

"Probably both," Marcus whispered back.

Leo thought about it. Then he nodded. "Respect."

After school, Marcus's dad was waiting by the front gate. Mrs. Rivera had called. Of course she had. "Mrs. Rivera says you told the truth today," Dad said. "Even when you didn't have to."

"Yeah."

"How'd that feel?"

"Hard," Marcus said. "And then *really* good."

Marcus didn't get a prize for telling the truth. He didn't get out of trouble completely. Mrs. Rivera was kind, but she still called his dad. The fish tank was still broken. Leo still got his yo-yo confiscated the next morning, which Leo felt was deeply unfair and said so several times. None of that disappeared. Honesty is not just about doing the right thing for other people. It's about not having to carry that weight around in your own chest. Lies are heavy. The truth is lighter than you think.

A PRAYER FOR YOU

God, being honest is harder than it looks. Sometimes the truth sits in my chest like a stone and the lie feels so much lighter. But You see both, and deep down I know which one You're waiting for. Give me the courage to raise my hand even when my arm feels heavy. Help me remember that the peace I feel after telling the truth is worth more than the comfort of staying quiet. And thank You for making a way back, every time I mess up. I want to be someone You'd be proud of. Amen.

THE HARDEST WORD AFTER UNFAIR

Noah had spent fourteen days on that poster board.

Fourteen. He had counted. He had a small calendar on his desk where he tracked important things, like how many days until his birthday and whether he'd remembered to feed the dog, and he had put a small star on every single day he worked on the History of Ancient Egypt project for Mr. Briggs's co-op class. Fourteen stars. Fourteen evenings of markers and index cards and his mom helping him spell "hieroglyphics" correctly, which took four attempts and a dictionary.

The poster had sections. It had color coding. It had a hand-drawn map of the Nile with a blue marker so carefully applied that Noah had given himself a cramp in his right hand that lasted two days. It had a timeline. A real one, with arrows.

He was, objectively, very proud of it.

Destiny's project was a single piece of paper.

Noah had seen it. One page, printed from the internet, with three sentences written at the bottom in pencil. The handwriting was tilted. There was no color. There was no timeline. There was, as far as Noah could tell, no Nile River.

Mr. Briggs gave Destiny an *A minus.*

He gave Noah a *B plus.*

BEFORE WE GO FURTHER...

have you ever worked really hard on something and had it feel like it didn't matter? Like someone who tried less got rewarded more? You don't have to tell anyone. But just notice that feeling in your chest right now. That's the feeling this whole chapter is about.

Noah sat at his desk in the church basement classroom and stared at his grade for a long time. Long enough that Mr. Briggs moved on to math. Long enough that everyone around him had flipped their folders and gotten out their pencils. Noah was still just sitting there with a look on his face that his mom would later describe as "the one that means something has gone deeply wrong."

Noah did not say anything in class.

He was saving it.

He carried it home on the bus, that specific, focused anger that sits very still and doesn't make noise. He managed to hold it together through the front door, through taking his shoes off, through his mom asking how his day was. “Fine," he said.

His mom looked at him the way moms look at you when they know perfectly well it's not fine and are simply deciding when to address it. She had a gift for this. It was, frankly, inconvenient.

He made it all the way to dinner before the volcano in his chest had something to say.

"Destiny got an A minus," Noah announced, to his macaroni.

"Okay," said Mom.

"Her project was one piece of paper."

"Okay."

"Printed from the internet."

"I see."

"Mine had a timeline." He looked up. "With arrows."

His mom set her fork down. "Do you want to talk about it or do you want to be annoyed about it?"

"*Both*," Noah said honestly.

> Feeling something and dealing with it aren't the same thing, and you're allowed to need a minute before you get from one to the other.

His mom let him be annoyed about it for two more days. This was something Noah appreciated about her. She didn't rush him into being fine. She gave him a reasonable amount of time to be unreasonable, and then she came and sat on the end of his bed on Wednesday evening with her Bible and a look that meant the window was closing.

"Have you heard of Joseph?" she asked.

"The one with the coat," Noah said, from under his pillow.

"The one with the coat," she confirmed. "His brothers sold him. Like, actually *sold* him. He ended up in prison for something he didn't do. And he was there for years, Noah. Years."

Noah emerged slightly from the pillow. "How many years?"

"A while."

"And he just forgave them?"

"Eventually. It wasn't instant. But yeah." She opened to the passage and read him a bit of it, not the whole thing, just enough. The part where Joseph sees his brothers again and doesn't destroy them, even though he could.

Noah thought about his poster board. With the arrows.

"That's different," he said. "He was in prison. I just got a B plus."

"You're right, it's different," Mom said. "But the bitterness works the same way."

Noah looked at the ceiling.

THE JOSEPH TEST:

Think of something unfair that happened to you. Now think of Joseph, who lost years of his life to unfairness and still came out without bitterness eating him alive. On a scale of one to ten, how much is your unfair thing still living rent-free in your head?

"The Bible often tells God's disciples to love and forgive." She paused. "It doesn't say 'only if they deserved it.'"

Noah had nothing to say to that. Which meant she was probably right.

He hated that.

> *Be kind to one another,*
> *tenderhearted, forgiving*
> *one another.*
> *Ephesians 4:32*

He prayed about it that night. "God, I worked really hard on that project and I don't think the grade was fair. I know I'm supposed to forgive Destiny *even though* she didn't really do anything to me, it's more Mr. Briggs actually, so maybe I need to forgive him. I don't know. This is complicated. Help."

He paused. "Amen."

He felt approximately fifteen percent better, which was not a lot, but was more than nothing.

The next morning he woke up and the volcano in his chest was quieter. Not gone. Quieter. The rumbling had dropped from a definite geological event to more of a minor inconvenience.

By Friday, something had shifted that Noah could not fully explain.

He still thought the grade was wrong. He was probably always going to think the grade was wrong. But carrying it around all week had not changed the grade, had not changed Destiny's A minus, had not changed Mr. Briggs's red pen one bit. It had just made Noah tired.

> Bitterness is like carrying someone else's backpack everywhere you go. It doesn't hurt them. It just makes your shoulders sore.

The next Tuesday at co-op, Destiny was showing her A minus to someone across the room and Noah walked past her table to sharpen his pencil.

He stopped.

This was not part of any plan.

"*Hey*," he said. "Good job on the project."

Destiny looked up. "Oh. Thanks."

That was it. Six words total, three each. No dramatic moment, no music, no feeling of golden light descending from the church basement ceiling, which had water stains and one flickering fluorescent tube that nobody had fixed since September.

But something let go.

Not everything. Not the part that still thought the timeline with arrows deserved better. But the hot, heavy part, the part that had been sitting in his chest since grade day, that part loosened its grip, just enough to breathe.

Noah sharpened his pencil and went back to his seat.

Mr. Briggs started class. Noah opened his notebook.

It was a regular Tuesday. And somehow, that felt like enough.

There is probably something you're still carrying. A grade, a game, a friend who didn't show up, a time someone got something you felt you deserved. You've been dragging it around and it has not gotten lighter. Here's what Noah figured out the hard way: letting it go doesn't mean it wasn't unfair. It absolutely might be unfair. It just means you decide to stop paying for someone else's mistake with your own peace. You only get so much energy. Spend it on something worth it.

A PRAYER FOR YOU

God, some things really are unfair, and I think You know that. So I'm not going to pretend I'm fine with everything. But I'm asking You to take the heavy part, the part that sits in my chest and makes me tired. Help me be like Joseph, who went through way worse than I ever have and still came out without bitterness owning him. I don't want bitterness to own me either. Help me say the kind word, even when I don't feel it yet. And maybe start with helping me mean it a little bit. Amen.

WIN THE RIGHT WAY OR NOT AT ALL

The crowd went absolutely wild.

And Josiah stood in the outfield with his glove in the air and the ball sitting inside it like a small, white, very complicated problem.

It had happened fast. Top of the ninth, two outs, bases loaded, the Riverton Rockets down by one and their best hitter sending a screaming line drive out to left-center. Josiah had run for it the way he always ran, all legs and no grace, the way his coach described as "enthusiastic but concerning." He'd lunged, glove out, and felt the ball smack into the leather with that specific, satisfying thwack that meant he'd actually done it.

The crowd erupted. His teammates erupted. Even the team parents who had been sitting in tense silence for three innings erupted.

Mr. Hendricks, the umpire, pumped his fist. "*Out*! Ball game!"

And Josiah knew, in the very specific way that your body knows things before your brain catches up, that his left foot had been over the foul line when he caught it.

Not by a lot. Maybe six inches.

But six inches is ... *six inches*.

QUESTION FOR YOU, RIGHT NOW:

If nobody saw it, does it still count? Like if a call happens and there are no umpires watching, did it still happen? Think about your actual answer. Not the one that sounds good. The real one.

The celebration was enormous.

Deon, the team captain, got to Josiah first, which meant Josiah got lifted approximately two feet off the ground by a ten-year-old who was built like a small refrigerator. Then the rest of the team arrived and it became a general pile of helmets and cleats and someone's elbow in Josiah's ear, which was fine, because winning a championship apparently made elbows irrelevant.

Josiah laughed and yelled and high-fived everyone who had a hand available. Because what else do you do when your team just won and the whole town is cheering and your coach is doing a victory dance that no adult should ever perform in public?

He was happy.

He was *mostly* happy.

There was a small, quiet part of him that was not happy at all, but he pushed it down somewhere near his cleats and decided to deal with it later.

Later turned out to be during the trophy ceremony.

Coach Martinez handed Josiah the trophy because he'd made the final catch. It was heavier than Josiah expected, gold-colored plastic on a black base with a little batter on top that didn't look like anyone in particular.

The crowd clapped. Someone's dad took seventeen photos in a row with a flash that was genuinely blinding.

Josiah held the trophy and smiled.

The quiet unhappy part climbed back up from his cleats.

> Doing the right thing when nobody's watching is easy to talk about. But it gets decided in public.

On the bus ride home, Josiah sat with the trophy in his lap and Deon next to him talking at approximately the speed of sound about the catch, the game, the season, the future, what they'd eat to celebrate, and whether Coach Martinez's victory dance could be considered a crime against humanity.

Josiah nodded at all of it.

"You good?" Deon said, finally noticing.

"Yeah," Josiah said. "Just tired."

Deon accepted this and kept talking. Josiah looked out the window at the fields going past and turned the trophy over in his hands and thought about six inches. Six inches of foul line. Six inches between what happened and what everyone thought happened.

It shouldn't feel this heavy. He'd won. His team had won. Mr. Hendricks hadn't seen it. Nobody had seen it. The game was over. The season was over. The trophy was real and in his hands and cold and solid and completely, thoroughly his.

Except.

Except his foot had been over the line.

Dinner at home was loud and celebratory. His dad grilled burgers. His brother wore his batting helmet for the entire meal, including dessert. His mom took more photos. His grandma called and talked for an hour and said "my champion" so many times Josiah lost count.

Josiah ate his burger and laughed at his brother and said "*thanks, Grandma*" in all the right places.

And the whole time, sitting right behind everything, quiet and flat and completely immovable, was the fact that his foot had been over the line.

He put the trophy on his desk when he went to bed. It caught the light from the hallway and gleamed in a way that was probably meant to look triumphant.

It did not look triumphant to Josiah.

It looked like a question he hadn't answered yet.

THE MIRROR TEST:

Here's something worth trying. Go stand in front of a mirror and say out loud: "I won that fair and square." If you can say it and completely mean it, you're good. If something in your face does a thing, that's useful information. Josiah couldn't pass the mirror test. Could you, for the things in your own life?

He did not sleep.

He tried. He was excellent at sleeping under normal circumstances, could drop off in approximately four minutes and had once fallen asleep during a thunderstorm, which his mother considered either impressive or alarming depending on the day.

He lay there and stared at the ceiling and thought about the catch from every possible angle, and no matter which angle he tried, his foot was still over the line. He thought about the Rockets' best hitter, who had gone back to his dugout thinking he'd hit a foul ball. He thought about their faces when the game ended.

He thought about Proverbs 10:9. Things you've heard in church show up without warning when you're lying in the dark trying not to think.

Walks securely. He turned that over. He was not feeling secure. He was feeling the opposite of secure. He was feeling like someone who had built something on ground that wasn't solid and was only now noticing the wobble.

At eleven-fifteen, he got up, went to his parents' room, and knocked.

His dad appeared in about four seconds, which meant he'd been awake too. Parents always knew.

"Can't sleep?" Dad said.

"My foot was over the line," Josiah said. “I didn’t win.”

His dad looked at him for a moment. Then he opened the door wider. "Come in. Tell me."

He told his dad everything. The catch, the foot, the line, the trophy ceremony, the bus ride, the mirror in his head he couldn't stop looking into. His dad listened without interrupting, which was something Josiah always appreciated.

When he finished, his dad sat quietly for a moment.

"What do you want to do?" Dad said.

"I want to tell Mr. Hendricks," Josiah said. "I think I have to."

"You know what that might mean."

"Yeah." Josiah looked at his hands. "I know."

"You still want to?"

Josiah thought about lying in bed staring at the ceiling. He thought about the trophy gleaming in the dark like a question. He thought about walks securely and what secure actually felt like and how it was the opposite of tonight. "Yeah," he said.

"We'll go in the morning."

Mr. Hendricks lived on Elm Street, twelve minutes from Josiah's house. He answered the door in a Saturday morning bathrobe holding a coffee mug, which was not how Josiah had pictured this going, but nothing about this situation had gone how Josiah pictured it.

Josiah told him. Straight, simple, no drama.

> The trophy didn't change. Josiah did. And that turned out to be the more important one.

Then he said, "Son, I've been umpiring Little League for eleven years. You're the first kid who's ever knocked on my door the morning after to give the trophy back."

Josiah didn't know what to say to that so he said nothing.

"The call stands. I can't go back and change a closed game. But I want you to know I heard you."

On the drive home, he held the trophy in his lap again. Same trophy. Same gold plastic. Same little batter on top who didn't look like anyone in particular.

Now, he could finally enjoy it.

There's probably something in your life that feels like that trophy. Something you're holding that should feel good but has a small, quiet problem attached to it. Maybe it's a grade, maybe it's a game, maybe it's something somebody thinks about you that isn't completely true and you haven't corrected. You don't have to fix it today. But you already know, don't you? The thing that keeps you from sleeping is usually the thing worth dealing with. Start there.

A PRAYER FOR YOU

God, I want to be someone who walks securely. Not perfectly, because I know I'm going to mess things up. But I want to be the kind of person who, when they mess up, goes and says so instead of hoping nobody noticed. Give me that kind of courage. The quiet kind, not the showy kind. The kind that knocks on someone's door on a Saturday morning in a bathrobe situation and says the true thing anyway. Help me care more about who I actually am than about what people think I am. Amen.

DO RIGHT WHEN IT COSTS YOU

The volcano was Micah's idea.

Not the volcano part, technically. Everybody does a volcano. The volcano is basically the macaroni art of science fairs. Perfectly acceptable, no real surprises, you mix the baking soda and vinegar, everyone politely says "ooh" and moves on to the solar system display.

Micah had done a volcano in second grade. It had been fine. It had erupted twice and then sort of wheezed.

No, what was Micah's idea was the lava color system.

He'd spent two weeks researching what different chemical combinations produced which colors, had tested five versions in his kitchen sink while his mom stood nearby with a dish towel and a look of cautious optimism, and had landed on a deep orange-red that looked, as his dad had said, "genuinely alarming in the best possible way."

Mrs. Park called the setup "one of the most visually impressive demonstrations I've seen at this level."

Owen had built the cone. The cone was good. Micah was not denying the cone.

But the lava color system was *Micah's.*

QUICK CHALLENGE:

Have you ever worked on something with someone and felt like your part didn't get noticed? Like the other person got the credit and you got the cleanup?

The science fair was on a Friday. Thursday evening, Micah was at home doing a final check of his notes when his phone buzzed with a message from Jordan, who was in their class and had a gift for knowing things she probably shouldn't know.

Did you see what Owen told Mrs. Park?

Micah stared at the message. *What do you mean?*

He went in after school and told her the lava color idea was his. Like, his whole presentation was about how he came up with it. She was suuuper impressed.

Science Fair Project

Micah read it twice. Then a third time, in case it changed.

It didn't change.

He sat on his bedroom floor with his notes in his lap and felt something rise in his chest that was not a named thing, not a clever label, just a hot, tight, breathless anger that started in his stomach and went all the way up to behind his eyes. He'd given up two Saturdays for those color tests. He'd ruined a perfectly good dish towel. His mom had found orange staining on the kitchen grout that they were still dealing with.

And Owen had walked into Mrs. Park's classroom after school and handed all of it over like it was his to give.

He confronted Owen the next morning, fifteen minutes before the fair opened, in the hallway outside the gym where their display was set up. Owen was fixing his name badge, which was a bold activity to be doing in that particular moment.

"Jordan told me what you said to Mrs. Park," Micah said.

Owen looked up. Something crossed his face, a quick thing, and then it was gone. "It was a group project. I was just explaining my contributions."

"You said the lava idea was yours."

"I said I developed it."

"Owen. I developed it. In my kitchen. For two weeks. My mom still has orange grout."

Owen straightened his name badge. "Look, we both worked on it. It's fine."

"It's not fine."

"Micah." Owen lowered his voice. "Mrs. Park already thinks it's mine. If you go in there and say something, you're going to look like you're just trying to make me look bad. Right before the fair. In front of everyone." He picked up his display board. "Just let it go."

He walked into the gym.

Micah stood in the hallway and tried to breathe through his fury. He had options. He'd already run through them by the time he got to his half of the display table.

> The hardest part of being wronged is figuring out what you do next.

Option one: walk straight to Mrs. Park right now, in front of everyone, and explain exactly what happened. Loud, clear, documented. Jordan could back him up. This option had a certain appeal.

Option two: say nothing. Let Owen have it. Go home and eat cereal and be quietly furious about it for the next several years.

Option three: something in between, which he couldn't quite see the shape of yet.

He spent the first forty minutes of the fair smiling at parents and explaining the lava flow system and saying "thank you" when they said it was impressive, and the whole time his brain was running the options on a loop like a broken record player.

Mrs. Park came by their table around the halfway mark. She looked at the volcano, looked at Micah, and said, "Owen told me quite a bit about your process yesterday. Very impressive thinking."

"Thank you," Micah said.

She started to move on. And then something happened that Micah had not planned, which was that his mouth opened. "Mrs. Park," he said, "could I talk to you for a minute? Privately. Not right now. Maybe after."

"Of course," she said. "Come find me after the judging."

THE QUIET PATH:

Think of a situation where someone wronged you and you had a chance to blow it up publicly but didn't. Or maybe you did blow it up and wish you hadn't. Either way: what would the quiet, right path have looked like?

The judging happened. Their volcano won second place in the physical sciences category, which meant a red ribbon and a handshake from the district science coordinator, who had a very firm grip and said "well done, young man" in a way that sounded like he said it approximately forty times per fair.

Owen accepted the ribbon. He held it up for his parents, who were photographing from the bleachers.

Micah clapped. Because what else do you do.

After the gym started emptying out, he found Mrs. Park at her desk in the corner where she'd been recording scores. He sat down in the chair across from her, and he told her.

Not dramatically. Not with Jordan as a witness, not with a list of evidence, not loudly. Just the straight version.

What he'd researched, what he'd tested, what the orange grout situation had cost his family, and what Owen had told her the afternoon before.

Mrs. Park listened with her pen down and her hands folded, which was how you knew she was actually listening and not just waiting for you to finish.

When he was done, she said, "Why didn't you say something this morning? Before the judging?"

Micah thought about it. "Because I didn't want to blow everything up. I figured if I told you now, you'd know. And whatever you do with it is up to you."

She leaned back, seeming to ponder this. Her eyes roamed around the table idly. Then she seemed to sit up.

Silently, she turned her desk calendar around so Micah could read it. The verse for that day read:

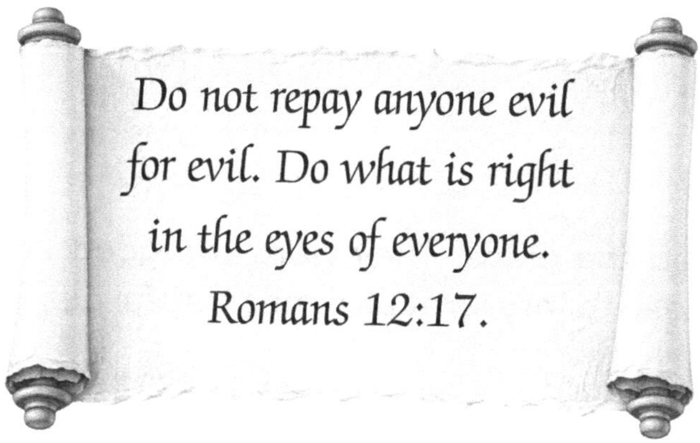

"I've had a desk calendar for three years," she said. "I read it when I'm deciding how to handle things." She looked at him steadily. "You just *lived* it."

Micah didn't find out exactly what Mrs. Park said to Owen. He never asked.

Owen came to school the following Monday and didn't quite meet Micah's eyes in the hallway, which told Micah something had been said.

On Tuesday, Owen set a bag of chips on Micah's desk when he walked in. No note. No explanation. Just chips.

Micah looked at them. Then at Owen, who had already sat down and was very busy with his backpack zipper.

Revenge feels good for about four minutes. Grace lasts forever. And it doesn't cost a thing you aren't okay losing.

He opened the chips. They were the good kind, which Micah chose to interpret as a meaningful gesture.

Let's face it. You're going to be Owen sometimes and Micah at others. The Owen moments are where you find out what kind of person you're becoming. And the Micah moments, the ones where you have every right to go nuclear and you choose the quieter door instead, those are the ones that build something in you. And they stick around long after the science fair is over and the ribbon is in a drawer and nobody remembers the volcano except you and your mom's orange grout.

A PRAYER FOR YOU

God, it is genuinely hard to do the right thing when the wrong thing feels so justified. When someone takes something that was mine and I want the whole world to know it, help me find the quieter door. Not because what happened was okay. It wasn't. But because I want to be the kind of person who trusts You to handle what I can't. You see everything, including the orange grout. Help me do right in the eyes of everyone, even when doing right feels like losing. Especially then. Amen.

SHOW UP UNTIL SOMETHING CHANGES

On the bright side, Ezra had a gift.

Unfortunately, the gift was not swimming.

The gift was, as far as he could tell, finishing last in a way that was so consistent it had stopped feeling like bad luck and started feeling like a personality trait.

Three meets. Three last places. Not close-last, not almost-last, but actual, definitive, everyone-is-already-out-of-the-pool-and-toweling-off last. At the second meet, a kid from the opposing team had started packing his swim bag before Ezra touched the wall.

Ezra had seen it happen. He had been unable to think of a single thing to say about it.

He was was the slowest swimmer at the Suncoast Swim Academy. This fact sat on his chest every single morning when he pulled on his swim cap and walked out to the pool deck and smelled the chlorine and thought, not for the first time, about how nice it would be to be doing literally anything else.

The cap, for the record, was bright orange. Coach Reyes issued them to every swimmer on the team. On faster swimmers, the cap looked sporty and professional. On Ezra, it looked like a warning label.

RIGHT NOW, BEFORE WE GO ON:

Have you ever been the worst at something you were still doing? Not just bad at it. The actual worst, measurably, with evidence? How did that feel? This whole chapter lives in that feeling.

The conversation with Coach Reyes happened on a Tuesday, after practice, when everyone else had gone and Ezra was still sitting on the bench by lane four with his goggles around his neck and his towel doing nothing useful.

Coach Reyes was a short, wide, extremely cheerful man who had the energy of someone who genuinely believed six AM practice was a privilege and not a punishment.

He had coached swimming for fifteen years and had the kind of deep, permanent tan that came from spending most of his life outdoors in Florida, and he always had a whistle and a clipboard and an opinion, usually all three at once.

He sat down next to Ezra on the bench. "Talk to me," he said.

"I want to quit," Ezra said. He'd been planning to ease into it but apparently his mouth had other ideas.

Coach Reyes nodded slowly. "Okay."

"That's it? *Okay*?"

"Quitting is always an option," Coach Reyes said. "I'm not going to tell you it isn't. This isn't the Olympics." He set his clipboard down. "But I want you to do one thing first."

Ezra looked at him sideways. "What?"

"Pray about it." Coach Reyes said it the way he said most things, directly, without making it weird. "Not for me. For you. Take it home tonight, put it in front of God, and see what comes back." He picked up his clipboard. "If you still want to quit tomorrow, I'll handle the paperwork myself."

Ezra did not know what to say to that so he said nothing, which was becoming a pattern.

> Quitting is always an option. The question is whether it's your option right now.

His mom was waiting in the pickup line in the blue minivan that had a dent on the rear bumper from the time she'd misjudged a parking structure and had never fully made peace with it. She looked at his face when he got in and said nothing for about thirty seconds, which was her version of reading the room.

"Bad practice?" she said finally.

"I told Coach I want to quit."

She pulled out of the parking lot. "And what did he say?"

"He said to pray about it."

She nodded like this was a *completely* reasonable response from a swim coach, which Ezra supposed it was, depending on the swim coach.

At home, he ate dinner and did homework and went through all the normal motions of a normal Tuesday evening, except that the quitting decision was sitting in the back of his head like a browser tab he couldn't close.

He'd already made up his mind, he was fairly sure. The prayer thing was just a formality.

He lay on his bed and stared at the ceiling and started to pray, which immediately felt like a conversation with someone who already knew what he was going to say.

"God," he said, "I'm going to quit swimming. I'm not good at it, and it's *embarrassing* and I'm tired. I just wanted to tell You."

5

He stopped. From his bookshelf, the spine of his Bible caught the light in a way that was probably coincidental.

He got up, got the Bible, and sat back on the bed.

FIND IT FIRST:

Before Ezra finds what he finds, here's a question. Think of someone from the Bible who looked like they were going to lose. Not someone who looked strong from the start. Someone who looked wrong for the job. Got one?

He wasn't looking for anything specific. He flipped to the middle and landed somewhere in First Samuel. His eyes moved across the page without much intention and then stopped, the way eyes do when something grabs them before the brain catches up.

David. The part before the Goliath fight, where Samuel is looking at all of Jesse's sons and keeps thinking he's found the right one and God keeps saying *no*. Big strong Eliab shows up and Samuel thinks surely this is the one, and God says *no, I don't look at what people look at. People look at the outside. I look at the heart.*

And then they send for David, who is out in the field watching sheep, because nobody had even bothered to bring him in. He wasn't in the lineup. He wasn't on anyone's team. He was the kid nobody thought to call.

Ezra read it twice.

Then he lay back and looked at the ceiling and thought about lane four and the orange cap and the kid packing his bag before Ezra had touched the wall.

David hadn't looked like a winner either.

He'd been the slowest one in the lineup. The one nobody expected. And God had looked at him anyway and seen something worth working with.

Ezra stared at the ceiling for a long time.

Then he went to sleep, which was a decision his body made before his brain finished the thought.

He went back to practice on Wednesday.

He didn't announce it. He just showed up, pulled on the orange cap, and got in lane four. Coach Reyes looked at him once and nodded once and that was the whole conversation.

The final meet of the season was three weeks later. Ezra had trained every day, which is the kind of sentence that sounds simple and is actually made of forty-five early mornings and a truly unreasonable amount of chlorine.

There was a card stuck to the inside of his swim bag that his mom had put there sometime in the second week without saying anything about it. He found it when he was looking for his goggles. Small card, her handwriting, one line:

> *Let us not become weary in doing good. At the proper time we will reap a harvest. Galatians 6:9.*

He left it in the bag. He looked at it every morning before he zipped it up.

The morning of the final meet, Ezra stood behind the block for the fifty-meter freestyle and looked at the pool. Lane four. Again. *Always* lane four.

The swimmers on either side of him were both faster. He knew their times. He had, in a moment of what he now recognized as unnecessary self-torture, looked up the heat sheets the night before.

He looked at the water. *I look at the heart.*

The starter beep went off. He dove.

He swam the way he'd been training, which was not the way he'd been swimming in September. Longer strokes, cleaner turns, his breathing in the pattern Coach Reyes had drilled into him until it became a reflex.

He touched the wall.

He looked up at the scoreboard, water in his eyes, breathing hard.

Fourth place.

Not first. Not second or third. Fourth. Out of eight. Dead center of the pack, on the right side of last. His personal best by four seconds.

He got out of the pool and his mom was already there at the barrier, which was logistically impressive given where the parent section was, and he walked straight into her and she put her arms around him and he cried. The kind that comes when something that was very hard is over and you made it through to the other side.

> You can either think
> "I'm not the best"
> or "this is my
> personal best."

Coach Reyes appeared at his shoulder. He didn't say anything for a moment. Then: "Told you to pray about it."

Ezra laughed, which came out half-cry, which was a new sound he hadn't made before. "Yeah. You did."

Fourth place doesn't sound like a victory. But Ezra knows something now that he didn't know in September. The scoreboard is not measuring how many six AM practices you showed up to when you didn't want to. It's not measuring the card in your swim bag or the prayer on a Tuesday night or the fact that you got back in lane four when you didn't have to. God's scoreboard measures different things. On that scoreboard, Ezra won by a lot.

A PRAYER FOR YOU

God, I don't always feel like the person You'd pick. Sometimes I feel like the kid nobody called in from the field, the one not even in the lineup. But You looked at David when nobody else did, and I thank You for looking at me too. Not at my times or my place or how I compare to everyone else. At my heart. Help me show up tomorrow even if today was hard. Help me not get weary. And when the harvest comes, help me recognize it for exactly what it is. Amen.

GIVE SO IT COSTS YOU EVERYTHING

Benjamin had been saving since September.

Not casually saving, not the kind where you put a dollar in a jar occasionally and feel good about yourself. Serious saving. *Documented* saving. He had a notebook, spiral-bound, blue cover, where he tracked every dollar and every source.

Three dollars for raking Mrs. Calloway's leaves. Five dollars from his birthday card from Uncle Terrence, who always sent exactly five dollars and had done so for as long as Benjamin could remember, with a card that said "buy yourself something nice" in handwriting that had never improved.

Two dollars for finding his dad's car keys, which his dad disputed as a legitimate earning opportunity but paid anyway because he was already late for work.

Seventy-three dollars and fifty cents, as of December twenty-third.

The game cost sixty-nine ninety-nine.

He had looked it up eleven times to confirm this, which was probably ten more times than necessary, but Benjamin was a careful person.

Tomorrow was Christmas Eve. The plan was to walk to the GameStop on Main Street with his mom in the morning, and purchase the game with his own money like a person who had planned and executed a financial strategy over four months. He would Christmas break doing exactly what he wanted in a way that felt completely and thoroughly earned.

It was a good plan. It was an excellent plan.

He went to sleep on December twenty-third feeling like someone who had their life together.

COUNT YOUR SAVINGS:

Do you have money saved up for something right now? Something specific you've been working toward? If yes, think about how long it took and what it cost you to save it. If no, think about something you really wanted and had to wait for.

Christmas Eve morning, it snowed with great commitment, and covered everything in about four inches by nine AM.

This made the walk to GameStop significantly less triumphant than Benjamin had pictured. He and his mom crunched down the sidewalk in boots, Benjamin with his notebook in his coat pocket, and arrived at GameStop at nine-fifteen to find it did not open until ten.

They waited in the car. His mom drank coffee from her thermos and listened to the radio. Benjamin watched the GameStop door with the patience of someone who had been preparing for this for four months.

At ten *exactly*, they went in.

The game was on the shelf. Right where it always was. Benjamin picked it up, turned it over, read the back for the eleventh time, and carried it to the register.

The total came to seventy-four dollars and thirty-nine cents with tax.

Benjamin's notebook said he had seventy-three fifty.

He stood at the register and did the math again, in case the math had changed. It had not changed.

He was *eighty-nine cents* short.

His mom, who had watched this development with the expression of someone who had suspected this might happen and had chosen not to mention it, opened her wallet and gave him a dollar. “Here you go.”

It was tempting. Very tempting.

> The best things you own are always the ones that cost you something to get.

But this heavily compromised the integrity of his financial strategy. “I’ll earn the money fair and square, Mom,” he said, swallowing his disappointment.

Christmas Eve in their house meant one tradition that was not negotiable, which was the evening service at the church their family had attended since before Benjamin was born. It was the one service a year where even his dad, who worked a lot and traveled more, was always there, in the good coat.

Benjamin liked the Christmas Eve service. They sang the old songs, which he knew all the words to. There were candles, and Pastor Nduka always told the Christmas story like it was the first time anyone had ever heard it, which somehow worked *every single time.*

He put the game on his desk before they left. Still in the bag. He looked at it once from the doorway. Then hHe put his coat on.

Pastor Nduka was a tall man with a deep voice and a laugh that started somewhere around his knees and worked its way up. He had a gift for making a church full of people feel like he was talking to each of them personally.

Benjamin had noticed this about him since he was small. It was a useful gift for a pastor. Slightly inconvenient if you were hoping to zone out during the sermon.

Tonight he did not get to zone out.

About halfway through the service, after the carols and before the candle lighting, Pastor Nduka set down his notes and looked out at the congregation with a different expression than the one he'd been wearing for the first half.

"I need to tell you about a family," he said.

Three nights ago. A house fire on Birchwood Drive. The Okafor family, who some people in the room would know from the Tuesday food pantry. Parents and four children, all safe, all out. But the house was *gone*, and everything in it. And Christmas morning was in eight hours.

"The children's ages are four, six, nine, and eleven," Pastor Nduka said. "I'm told the nine-year-old had been saving up for a video game."

Benjamin went very still.

"We're passing a basket," Pastor Nduka said. "Whatever you can give tonight goes directly to this family. No administration, no processing time. Tonight."

The baskets came out. Levi, who was sitting next to Benjamin in the wool sweater he hated, tugged on his sleeve. "Are we going to give?" he whispered.

He had approximately seventy-five cents in his coat pocket at any given time, in a miscellaneous collection of coins, and was always prepared to deploy them.

Benjamin looked at the basket coming down the row.

STOP HERE.

What would you do? Not what you should do. What would you actually do? Nobody's watching. Be honest with yourself. Seriously, close the book for ten seconds and think about it.

He thought about the game on his desk. The bag. The receipt. The notebook with four months of documented earnings. The dollar from his mom. The eighty-nine cents.

He thought about a nine-year-old on Birchwood Drive who had been saving up for a video game and whose house was gone.

The basket reached their row.

Levi put in his seventy-five cents with great seriousness, both hands, like he was completing an important transaction.

The basket moved to Benjamin. He put his hand in his coat pocket.

His fingers found the folded bills, the seventy-three fifty that represented September through December, the leaves and the birthday card and the car keys and all of it.

He thought about the game on the desk. He thought about the nine-year-old. He thought about something his grandma had embroidered on a pillow that sat on her sofa that he had read approximately four hundred times over his life during family visits because it was right at eye level when you sat in the armchair:

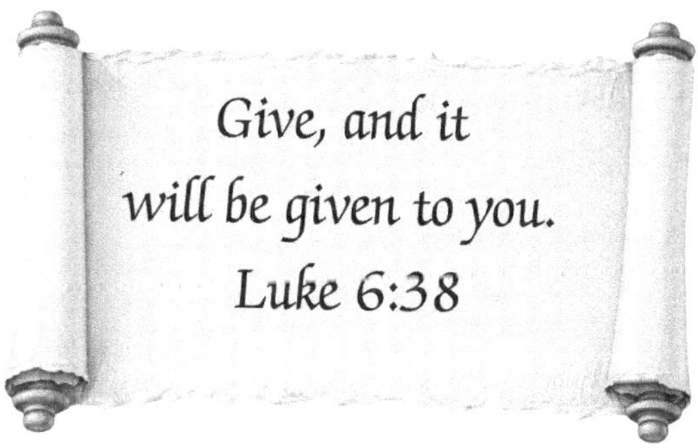

She put it on the pillow because she wanted it to be the first thing people read when they sat down in her house. He'd always thought it was just a pillow.

He pulled out the money.

His hand made the decision before his brain finished the argument, and he put sixty dollars in the basket and held the remaining thirteen fifty in his lap and passed the basket to the next person.

Levi looked at him with round eyes. "Was that your game money?"

He couldn't quite say the words out loud. "Some of it."

Levi thought about this with the gravity of a six-year-old processing a large concept.

Benjamin sat in the second pew from the left in the good coat and held his thirteen fifty and felt something in his chest that he had no word for. Not happy exactly. Not sad. Something bigger than both of those.

> Sixty dollars lighter,
> and somehow fuller
> than he'd ever been.

On Christmas morning, there was a small envelope under the tree with his name on it. Inside was a gift card from his grandma. *GameStop. Seventy-five dollars.*

He sat on the living room floor and held it for a long time. Then he laughed and wept. It was a reasonable response.

Benjamin didn't know about the gift card. He gave sixty dollars into a basket on Christmas Eve with no expectation of getting anything back. That's the only version of this story that works, because if he'd known, it wouldn't have cost him anything. Generosity only counts when it's real, when it actually costs you something you wanted. You already know what generosity that real feels like, because you know what it would cost you. That's the point. That's always been the point.

A PRAYER FOR YOU

God, it's hard to give things away. Especially things I worked for, saved up for, planned for. My hands want to hold on. So I'm asking You to help me open them. Not because I'll get something back, even though You promise I will, but because holding everything tight gets exhausting and I don't want to live like that. Help me see the basket when it passes. Help me think about the nine-year-old on Birchwood Drive before I think about myself. Amen.

BE THE FIRST ONE TO BREAK THE SILENCE

Camp Ridgeline had a rule about competitions.

The rule was posted on a laminated sign outside the main lodge, in letters large enough to read from a reasonable distance, and it said:

All camp competitions are friendly. Friendly means we win with grace and lose with dignity. Violations of the friendly competition rule will result in one full hour of kitchen duty, which involves the industrial dishwasher, which is loud and damp and generally unpleasant.

Tobias had read this sign approximately fourteen times over three summers at Camp Ridgeline. He had always considered himself a friendly-competition kind of person. He was going to have strong feelings about this assessment later in the week.

The competition in question was the Ridgeline Relay, which happened every year on Wednesday afternoon.

Despite the laminated sign, it was taken with a seriousness that the sign probably hadn't anticipated.

It was four events: a foot race, a canoe sprint, a climbing wall section, and a trivia round at the end, and the winning cabin got a trophy that was a wooden bear holding a small flag, which sounds undignified but was actually considered a significant honor at Camp Ridgeline and Tobias had wanted it for two summers.

Tobias was in Cabin Seven. Jordan was his best friend and his bunkmate and the person he'd requested to be cabinmates with specifically, which required a form, which Tobias had submitted in May.

Jordan was, as it turned out, in Cabin Eight this year, because the form had been processed incorrectly, which nobody discovered until arrival day, which was too late.

This was, in retrospect, relevant information.

QUICK ONE:

Think about your best friend. Now imagine being on opposite teams against them in something you both really wanted to win. Could you keep it friendly? Like, genuinely?

We'll see how Tobias does.

The first three events went fine. Tobias's Cabin Seven won the foot race by half a second. Jordan's Cabin Eight won the canoe sprint by a lot, because Jordan was a strong paddler and Tobias's canoe partner Marcus had the technique of someone who had never seen water before. The climbing wall was a draw, which satisfied nobody.

It all came down to trivia.

Tobias was good at trivia. Jordan was also good at trivia. This had never been a problem before because they had always been on the same team, which meant their combined trivia power was effectively unstoppable, and they had won seventeen rounds of trivia between them over two summers without ever being divided.

Divided, it turned out, was different.

The trivia round had ten questions and a buzzer system that the camp director had ordered online and which worked about seventy percent of the time. The score was tied at four-four going into the final two questions.

Question nine: *what is the tallest mountain in North America?*

Jordan buzzed first. "Denali."

Correct. Cabin Eight led five to four.

One question left. Everything on it. Tobias looked at his buzzer. His hand was sweating in a way he found embarrassing and could not stop.

CABIN 7: 5
CABIN 8: 5

In what year did the first man walk on the moon?

Tobias's hand slammed the buzzer before the question finished. "1969."

Correct.

Five-five. Tiebreaker.

The tiebreaker question was about state capitals, which Tobias had studied specifically because his dad was the kind of person who quizzed state capitals on long car rides and Tobias had retained all of it.

He buzzed before Jordan. He answered correctly. He won.

Cabin Seven erupted.

Tobias stood up and something came out of his mouth in the general chaos of the moment that he would spend the next seventy-two hours wishing he could take back.

He looked at Jordan across the table and said, loudly enough for half the lodge to hear: "You're not as smart as you think you are."

Jordan looked at him. One long, flat look, the kind that doesn't need words because it's doing something words can't do. Then he picked up his score sheet, put it down, and walked out of the lodge.

Tobias stood with the rest of Cabin Seven celebrating around him and felt the win go flat in approximately two seconds, like a soda left open overnight.

He'd meant something like: *finally got you.* A trash-talk thing, the kind that's supposed to be funny between best friends. That's what he'd meant. That was not what had come out.

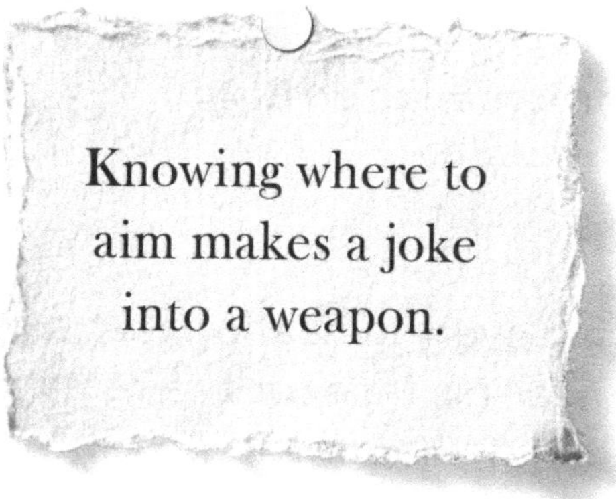

That night, Cabin Seven was celebrating with contraband gummy bears that someone's mom had packed in a sock. Tobias ate two and tasted nothing.

Jordan's bunk was three feet from his. Jordan was reading a book with the focused attention of someone who was definitely not reading, just holding a book near his face as a social boundary.

Tobias opened his mouth twice. Both times he closed it.

He fell asleep without saying anything.

Day two was worse. The thing about a silence between two people who are in the same twelve-foot cabin is that it fills up the entire twelve feet. It had a presence. It sat on the bunk ladder and waited in the bathroom line and ate across from you at every meal. It was heavier than any actual object in the cabin, including Marcus's inexplicably enormous duffel bag.

Tobias knew he was wrong. He had known since approximately four seconds after the words came out of his mouth. The wrongness was not the question. The question was whether he was going to be the one to walk across the twelve feet first, or whether he was going to wait for Jordan to do it.

Jordan was not doing it.

Jordan was giving every indication that he was prepared to read books near his face for the remaining four days of camp and then go home and possibly never address this directly for the rest of their lives.

Tobias found this deeply inconvenient.

THE GRUDGE QUESTION:

Have you ever waited for someone else to apologize first when you knew you were the one who should go first? Maybe saying sorry first feels like losing something. That feeling has a name. It's called pride. And it is one of the most expensive things you will ever hold onto.

Brother Pete found Tobias on the dock on Thursday afternoon.

Brother Pete was Camp Ridgeline's senior counselor, which meant he had been doing this for twelve years and had seen every version of every cabin conflict and was not remotely impressed by any of them, but also genuinely cared about each one, which was a combination Tobias found both reassuring and slightly terrifying. He was a big man with a short beard and a Camp Ridgeline staff shirt that had been washed so many times the logo was mostly a memory.

He sat down next to Tobias on the dock without preamble and looked at the lake.

"You and Jordan," he said.

"Yeah," Tobias said.

"What happened?"

Tobias told him. All of it, including the part where he knew it was mean when he said it, which he hadn't admitted out loud yet. Brother Pete listened to all of it without making a face.

"Here's a question," Brother Pete said, when he was done. "Who needs to be right more: you, or the friendship?"

Tobias looked at the lake. A duck was crossing it with great confidence, which Tobias found mildly annoying given the circumstances.

"He hasn't come to me," Tobias said.

"He's not the one who said it."

Tobias had nothing for that. It was just true, sitting there on the dock, not dressed up as anything.

Brother Pete stood up and stretched and said, in the same tone he might use to mention the weather: "There's a thing in Matthew, chapter five, about leaving your gift at the altar and going to sort things out with your brother first. Before anything else. First." He looked at Tobias. "The friendship is the gift. Figure out what you're waiting for."

He walked back up the dock. The duck finished crossing the lake and disappeared into the reeds.

Tobias sat for another few minutes. Then he got up.

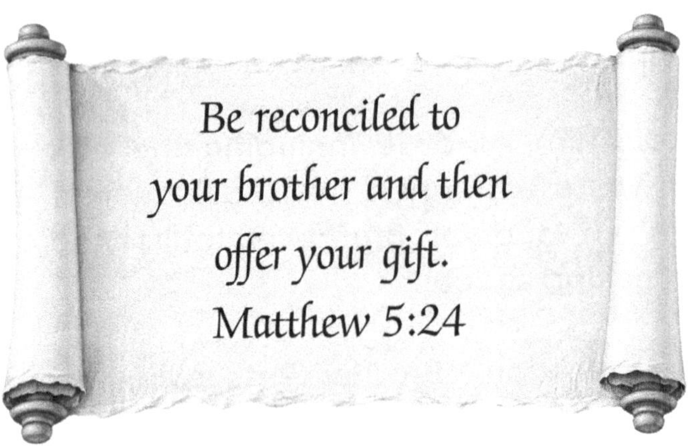

He knocked on Jordan's bunk frame at nine-fifteen, which was lights-out minus fifteen minutes, which gave him a specific and finite window before Brother Pete came through and shut things down.

Jordan looked up from his book-that-wasn't-being-read.

> Going first is not losing. Going first is the whole point.

"I said something mean," Tobias said. "On purpose. I knew where it would land and I said it anyway because I was excited that we won, and that's not an excuse, that's just what happened. I'm sorry."

Jordan looked at him for a moment.

"It was really mean," Jordan said.

"Yeah, I know. I’m sorry."

Another moment.

"Okay," Jordan said. He moved his book. "Sit down."

Tobias sat on the edge of the bunk. Marcus, across the cabin, was doing of a terrible job of pretending to sleep.

"I was going to come to you eventually," Jordan said.

"I know," Tobias said. "I didn't want to wait for eventually."

Tobias was wrong. The hard part isn't knowing. The hard part was crossing the twelve feet. And Jordan would have gotten there eventually. Probably. But eventually is a long time to sit in a twelve-foot cabin with a silence that has its own presence and eats at every meal with you. The first move costs you something. Pride, mostly. But pride is a bad thing to be protecting in the first place, and losing it turns out to be a relief. The friendship was on the other side of twelve feet. It always was.

A PRAYER FOR YOU

God, I know who I need to go to. I've known for a while. I've just been waiting for them to come first, which is its own kind of answer. Help me put down whatever I'm protecting and cross the distance. Not because I'm sure how it'll go. Not because I know they'll say okay. But because You said go first, before anything else, and I think You said it because You knew this exact situation was coming. Give me the words. Or even just the knock. I can handle the rest from there. Amen.